Northumberland at the Turn of the Century

Girl returning from an errand to the greengrocer

NORTHUMBERLAND
at the turn of the Century

edited by

Robin Gard

ORIEL PRESS

© 1970 Northumberland Local History Society.

First Published 1970.

ISBN   O   85362   100   4.

Library of Congress Catalogue Card Number 78-129644.

PUBLISHER'S NOTE
The illustrations in this book are reproduced from old photographs some of them faded sepia, and they should not be judged by modern photographic standards.

Published by
ORIEL PRESS LTD.
32 Ridley Place,
Newcastle upon Tyne England NE1 8LH.
Text set in 10 on 11 point Plantin.
Title pages in Gloucester.
Printed by Tyne Printing Works Newcastle.

ACKNOWLEDGEMENTS

One of the objects of the Society in sponsoring this book was to involve as many of its members as possible in a single enterprise. The response was extremely gratifying and so many people have helped in one way or another that the first thanks of the Society must go to its members at large. The Committee particularly thanks Mrs. E. W. Mitchell (President) for contributing the Introduction and Mr. R. M. Gard for arranging the photographs and writing the commentary, aided and counselled by Mr. R. A. S. Cowper (Chairman), Miss F. Harland and Mr. A. I. Buchanan, comprising the editorial sub-committee. The book could not possibly have been published without professional and material assistance, and the Society gratefully acknowledges the practical encouragement given by Mr. Bruce Allsopp of Oriel Press, the generous financial aid lent by four members of the Society and, not least, the secretarial and other services of the County Record Office.

The Northumberland Local History Society was formed in 1966 to draw together the many groups and individuals interested in learning more about the history of Northumberland. Twice a year it issues a newsletter informing members of the activities of its affiliated local history societies, it promotes projects on which these societies can combine to record neglected aspects of county history, it arranges country meetings to encourage its members to explore less familiar parts of the county, and it aims to sponsor publications to enable them to study local history with greater knowledge, purpose and pleasure. Applications for membership and for information should be sent to the Secretary, B. Long, F.S.A. Scot, Lewie Cottage, Kielder, Hexham.

CONTENTS

ILLUSTRATIONS

CREDITS

The Society is grateful to all those who kindly lent or otherwise made available the several thousand original photographs, prints, postcards, glass plates, slides and negatives from which the final selection was made, and thanks in particular to the following persons and institutions for permission to reproduce the photographs used:—

Mrs. M. Anderson: 98,99; R. Aln & Breamish History Society: 16,77; Bedlington Co-operative Society: 14, 65, 66; R. G. Bolam: 32; Mrs. Bolton: 97; the late G. Robinson: 76; Miss Charlton: 67,70,73,78,82,104; Sir John Craster: 55; Mrs. Davison: 79; J. Day: 36; Mrs. W. Fry: 92; R. J. A. Gazzard: 75; E. P. Griffith: 24; Miss M. Howey: 74; W. Lockey: 15, 44-49, 51, 84, 103; T. Long: 50; E. Mansfield: 4, 63, 64; R. Murray: 23, 37, 93-96, 100, 102; Newcastle upon Tyne Central Library: 8, 12, 18-22, 52-54, 58, 60, 72; Northumberland Record Office: 5-7, 9, 13, 25, 27, 28, 30, 38-40, 68, 69, 71, 81, 83, 88, 89 (Mitford Collection); 29, 35, 86; Prudhoe Library: 11; Society of Antiquaries of Newcastle upon Tyne: frontispiece, 1-3, 10, 17, 26, 31, 33, 34, 41-43, 56, 57, 59, 61, 85, 87, 90, 91, 101, 105; South Shields Central Library: 62, 80.

INTRODUCTION

by Ellen W. Mitchell, *President of the Northumberland Local History Society.*

This is the first publication of the Northumberland Local History Society. We organised ourselves less than four years ago with the simple aims of stimulating the interest of the ever-increasing number of people keen to learn about the history of our county and to help them in their work.

There are thriving societies in many areas and we are helping to establish more. Hundreds of members are enjoying learning from talks during the winter sessions and from outings to places of historic interest in the summer months.

One cannot but be conscious of history in Northumberland. The evidence is all about us, in castles and churches, in our villages and towns, their names, their fields and pathways. But all of these are open to siege – the siege of time and the newer threat of modern development. Progress all too often means demolition; we must aim, wherever necessary, to preserve and if that is not practicable, to record.

Those of us who have lived more than fifty years, have lived through social change so great that revolution is not too strong a word to apply to it. In that time we have accepted as part of our lives electric lighting, the vacuum cleaner, the electric washing machine and refrigerator, radio and television, the permanent wave and the electric blanket. We live in centrally heated houses and travel by car and aeroplane. Above all we have become an affluent society and the majority of people enjoy a standard of living undreamed of at the turn of the century. Perhaps the invention of television might be less of a surprise to a miner of 1900, could he see it, than the simple fact that a miner of today can own one.

But when new things come, old things go. We have seen the last of the poss-stick on washing day, the hot brick or the oven-shelf wrapped in flannel to warm the bed, the street lamp-lighter and in the countryside the happy rides on the hay-bogies.

I remember as a child riding in a trap and handing the toll-money to the woman at the toll-house on the Barrington to Choppington road, riding to Bedlington Hoppings in a horse-drawn brake and cycling to Morpeth on my first bicycle to see the ' hirings '.

But memories die with every generation. We must, therefore, seek out and preserve the hidden evidence of our personal past – old letters, bills, leases, costume, records of old customs and above all, the photograph.

Once it is accurately dated, the photograph becomes a valuable historic record and it has the advantage of having almost universal appeal. It seldom fails to produce immediate reactions of interest, curiosity, reminiscence, nostalgia and entertainment. It records the passing scene in any generation but it is uniquely valuable to us in illustrating the life of the pre-cinema, pre-television era and will remain one of our greatest sources of social history material for that age which ended with the First World War.

This book is about that era. It is not only an interesting collection of pictures; it is an historical document.

There must be hundreds of photographs as valuable as these lying hidden away, forgotten or unappreciated. It is high time they were collected. Perhaps this book is just a beginning.

The Society would welcome your help in identifying any of the people and places we have been unable to name.

CHILDREN

Memory happily recalls only the sunshine hours of childhood and mercifully fails to record the many frustrations of growing up, the endless waiting for this or that to happen, the indignity of having to wear old fashioned or handed down clothes, the pain of neglect, of the sharp word or heavier hand. As for school, who does not remember more clearly the welcome sound of the afternoon bell than the laborious hours of copying, chanting tables, reciting, sewing, or just listening and fidgetting in the long bench desks.

Although the holidays were then, just as now, mostly spent in whiling away the empty days, playing with friends next door, kicking a football on the green, running errands or getting up to mischief, it is the highlights which stand out in the memory, the week at the seaside or on the farm, the outings to Whitley Bay, the annual visit to grandma or aunty in the country, a jolting ride on the hay waggon, the excitement of the fair, or the very special shopping expedition to Newcastle.

1. With no television, cinema, radio and few organised activities, opportunities for entertainment were limited and children just had to amuse themselves. Doubtless, the experience of being photographed tickled the fancy of this happy group of children at Holystone, about 1900.

2. A boy proudly wheels his toy engine before a young admirer and a more critical, barefooted, spectator while other children gather round the sweet shop in The Side, Newcastle.

3. Children passing the time of day on the pavement in Sandgate, Newcastle. Most of the children in this and the picture above are wearing hats and layers of clothes.

4. Cambo schoolroom, about
1890. By the time this remarkable photograph was taken
the practice of teaching
children of all ages simultane-
ously in one large schoolroom
was already out-moded. The
teacher, Miss Ellen Richardson,
with the assistance of only one
pupil teacher, has charge of some
70 children. The walls are
covered with an interesting
display of charts and other
visual aids.

5. Mitford school children,
1912. All generations will
recognise the elementary
experiment in telegraphy. At
this time all children, except the
very poor, wore stout boots or
clogs, the boys' boots well
hobnailed to last.

Coronation day 1911 Childrens Tea

6. Saying grace before the Coronation Day children's tea party at Mitford, 1911. Unfortunately, the heavy road traffic of today makes it impossible to arrange the popular street tea parties formerly held on public occasions.

7. Paddling in the Wansbeck at River Green, about 1910.

Since the children are clearly wearing their best clothes, girls in their white frocks and straw hats, and boys in jackets, waistcoats and breeches as well as the inevitable cap, the scene is probably a Sunday School outing.

HOUSE AND HOME

Up to the middle of the nineteenth century the majority of ordinary folk in the north east, at any rate, lived in very primitive conditions, whole families eating and sleeping in one or two rooms, whether in farm cottage or pit row, the main room heated by an open fire which was the only means of cooking, lighted mainly by oil lamp, and without indoor water or sanitation. The two storey four roomed terraced houses which by the turn of the century had sprawled over the urban landscapes of Tyneside, Blyth, Ashington and other towns did at least provide room for parents and children to sleep apart, while the gradual introduction of gas lighting and tapped water, and eventually the water closet, began to make domestic life more comfortable. This was the heyday of the cold and airless front parlour, reserved only for the special occasions, but home was the hearth before the warm glow of the range in the back parlour, the table alternately covered with sewing, ironing and other domestic work, but how readily cleared for the oil cloth to be spread with cups, plates and cutlery from handy dresser or kitchen press.

8.   Fishermen's cottages at Newbiggin on Sea.

Cottages whether for fishermen, pitmen, or farm labourers were usually built in rows or squares.   The routine of domestic life in such close quarters was carried out practically in public, but the same conditions bred the strong sense of community which marks the Northumberland village character.

9. Mitford Manor House kitchen.

The dog wheel in the corner used for turning the spit must have been extremely rare even seventy years ago but in recording it the photographer has also left a vivid impression of the way in which Victorians fondly crowded the walls and mantel-shelves of their living rooms, whether grand or humble, with treasured ornaments.

10. Interior of Stephenson's Cottage, Wylam.

George Stephenson was born here in 1781. Now known as Street House and maintained by the National Trust, the cottage was then a two storied house let off in four single roomed apartments. This photograph was taken in 1910 but preserves the character of a typical workman's cottage in the 19th century.

11. Village oven, Prudhoe.
Women baking their weekly
bread at the communal oven,
Prudhoe. The loaves were
usually baked in the pan rather
than as cottage or flat loaves.
The woman wielding the shovel
wears a man's cap, a very
common habit in pit
villages.

12. Upturned boats, known
as mules, used as houses on
Newbiggin on Sea beach.

SHOPPING

Shopping seventy years ago was on the whole a very leisurely business affording plenty of time and opportunity for pleasant social gossip. It certainly took time in the shop itself, time for sugar, rice, peas, lentils to be weighed and packed in blue paper bags, for butter to be slapped and shaped, for ham to be sliced by hand, time to rest on the high shop chairs while the pennies and farthings were totted up, for money to be sent by express aerial container and for the change to come rattling back along the wires – time enough indeed for gossip!

Although the emporiums of Newcastle could provide practically everything from a pin to a glass candelabra, most trades had their own windows so that the haberdasher, draper, milliner, ironmonger, grocer and many others, all had to be visited to complete a modest shopping list, while many goods or kitchen wants were supplied by door to door salesmen. And then there were the street stalls on market days or at the hoppings when anything from fruit, vegetables, ribbons, pots, pans, kitchen gadgets, shoes, shirts to bric-a-brac and useless ornaments could be acquired without ceremony.

13. A street hardware dealer attracts a crowd in the corner of Morpeth Market Square, the scene being viewed with interest by a young housewife and her children and with more detachment by a senior citizen, about 1905.

14. Bedlington Co-operative Society grocery shop.

This picture, obviously taken to advertise the most up to date shop interior, betrays a standard of formal service far removed from the modern self service store.

15. Street stalls at Bedlington Hoppings.

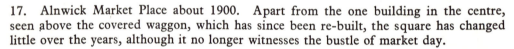

16.   Alwin Hill market, for the weekly sale of butter, cheese and eggs, held at the foot of the road leading up to Kidlandlee where the Allerhope Burn joins the River Alwin.

17.   Alnwick Market Place about 1900.   Apart from the one building in the centre, seen above the covered waggon, which has since been re-built, the square has changed little over the years, although it no longer witnesses the bustle of market day.

THE TOWN

Although they share the common heritage of a border county, no two towns or villages in Northumberland are alike. Even today the buildings and streets, when freed from the incessant motor traffic, still clearly witness many of the historical factors which have determined their individual character. Gone for ever, however, and at what great cost to the community spirit, is the time when the high street itself was a meeting place for a quiet conversation or a leisurely stroll.

18.   Marygate, Berwick upon Tweed, on probably a fairly quiet day, even for 1900.

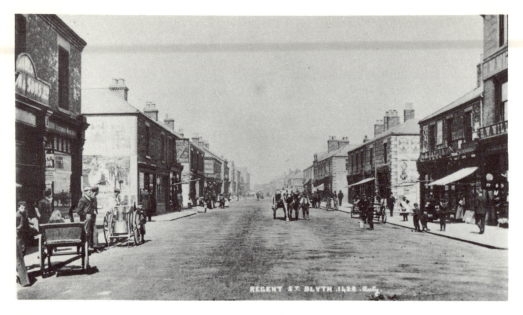

19. Regent Street, Blyth, in the days when advertisements appeared on every available wall. The large poster seen immediately above the milk churn cart announces a performance of the melodrama " The Old Toll House " at Blyth's Theatre Royal.

20. Newgate Street, Morpeth. The genteel country town atmosphere of Morpeth where buildings of various periods seem to like living together contrasts strikingly with the severely functional and regimented aspect of Regent Street, Blyth, built mostly at one period in the late nineteenth century.

21. The imposing buildings of Market Street, Newcastle upon Tyne, with this famous shop frontage could have left the visitor in no doubt that Newcastle was the metropolis of the North East. Among many points of interest is the variety of lamp standards, including the store's own exterior window lighting.

22. Newgate Street, Newcastle upon Tyne, a street of no great pretensions but alive with the bustle of commerce and the continual clatter of traffic, now also including the first noisy motor cars.

23. Rothbury about 1880. Although not a particularly clear picture, this gives a good impression of the leisurely pace of life in the country town in Victorian England. The thatched building at the end of the street was the " Three Half Moons ", on the site of which the Council Offices and Newcastle Hotel were later built.

24. Battle Hill, Hexham, decorated with the flags of all nations on the occasion of Queen Victoria's Jubilee, 1897.

THE LAND

In the early years of the century almost ten thousand people, a quarter of them women, worked full time on the land, and agriculture was still the only way of life known to the majority of country folk.   Each village and even many of the larger farms were able to supply most of their own basic needs and, despite the large scale yearly movement of the farm hinds after the May hirings, managed to preserve a strong sense of community. Soon, new machinery would cut out the need for a large labour force and the labourers who remained would become skilled workmen, able by means of easy motor transport to enjoy the amenities of the town.   By 1914 the old isolation, independence and traditional way of country life had gone for ever.

25.   Casting a ridge, near Mitford.

26.   Hoeing at Kirknewton. In former times the Northumberland farm labourer as a condition of his yearly hiring agreement had to provide a woman worker, commonly known as a *bondager*, for harvest and other farm work, and the practice continued well into the present century.

Although Northumberland was, as it still is, predominantly a live stock county, it is by the calendar of arable cultivation, from the first ploughing of the stubble to the final harvest, and particularly the sight and sound of men and horses toiling together in the field, that older people recall country life.

27.   Mowing at Mitford.

The high pointed horse collars, here decorated with brasses, were peculiar to Northumberland.

28.   The hay wain.

In the old days all heavy carts and waggons had to have large broad wheels to avoid rutting the unmade country roads and farm tracks.

29. Stacking hay at Castle Heaton, about 1910.

The long haystack was once a notable feature of the Northumberland farm scene. Stacks commonly measured sixteen yards by five yards at the base, and when they reached beyond pitchfork height, the hay was raised by means of a rope, pole, jib and grab.

The picture shows the pike of hay falling from the grab, the horse drawing the rope standing at its fullest distance. Two stackers and six women are on the stack which would eventually be twice as high.

30. Sheep washing below Mitford Bridge, about 1910.

The sheep were washed before clipping to remove grease and cleanse the wool, so as to obtain a better price at market.

31. Sheep shearing. The shearers would probably travel round the country districts and be hired by the farmer, his own hinds and bondagers acting as auxiliary labour.

32. Rothbury sheep auction, about 1875.
The permanent pens at Rothbury Mart were built about 1878 so that this photograph showing the traditional auction ring must have been earlier. The figure in white in the centre is Samuel Donkin, the well-known auctioneer. Although the importance of the sale is attested by the attendance of about 200 farmers and dealers, their immediate interest is obviously focused on the local photographer, J. Worsnop, who in order to achieve this remarkable bird's eye view must have had to climb on to the roof of a neighbouring house, or possibly up a tree.

33. Waiting for the reaper.
The woman is wearing the traditional bondager's costume of a straw bonnet over a scarf tied round the head to protect the complexion, a blue blouse and pink kerchief, and a coarse woollen skirt. Black stockings and hobnailed boots usually completed the attire.

34. Many of the older workers seeing this new reaper and binder in the harvest field about 1910 would remember the days when corn was still cut by sickle and gathered and bound by hand, while the young ones would live to see the combine become common-place.

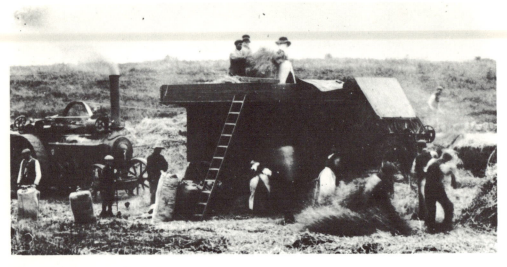

35. Threshing at Castle Heaton about 1910.
By this time steam traction engines, ploughing machines, and threshers, cumbersome as they were, had already proved the economy of mechanisation and the first tractors were on the way which would eventually render the working horse obsolete.

36. Fowler 12 h.p. single cylinder cable ploughing machine, one of a pair built in 1872, with harrow and cultivator in tow, photographed in 1913 at Willington Farm where it worked until 1935. Steam ploughing was widely practised before the first world war, but because of the expense of maintaining the heavy machines the work was usually contracted out to large agricultural contractors such as the Northumberland Steam Cultivation Company formed in 1870.

COUNTRY WORK

At one time most of the larger villages would have included a blacksmith, joiner, mason, shoemaker, tailor, and miller. It is possibly because their work was so commonplace that it seems to have interested few of the early photographers so that hardly any photographs have been found of these everyday crafts and occupations. The same applies to brick and tile making, limeburning, implement making, woollen manufacture, quarrying, stone dressing, iron founding, paper making, brewing, bonnet making and numerous local industries and trades which provided work in the country towns.

37. William Orr, miller of Thrum Mill, Rothbury.

38. Mitford smithy about 1910. James Berkley at work watched by Thomas Blair, the estate bailiff, while an unidentified man, possibly a railway worker, seems more interested in the camera.

39. Hauling timber in Mitford woods.

40. Mitford estate sawmill, about 1910, with Robert Brown, the estate carpenter, superintending operations.

41. The flitting.

The Northumberland farm worker was normally engaged at the local hirings for one year from May to May. Among his conditions were a free cottage, coals, grazing, hay and straw for one cow, barley and wheat for bread, 1000 yards of potatoes, as well as a yearly wage and rates for the bondager he supplied. Although many workers probably stayed with one farmer for years, it was quite usual for many more to move to another farm and the general exodus which took place was known as the flitting.

42. Girl gathering driftwood, Upper Coquetdale.

43. Coquetdale shepherd.

COAL MINING

When these photographs were taken Northumberland had as many as eighty pits and almost forty thousand miners worked at full stretch to produce more coal than ever before or since. Conditions were poor and work hard: the skill, strength and sometimes the spirit of the miner was wasted in working thin seams by hand for long hours and poor pay. Only the determined grasped the meagre opportunities for improvement which school, chapel, institute or Union lodge could offer: for the rest it was down the pit at 13 years. Life was never easy but hardships were shared and dangers, even tragedy, accepted. Each village was a close community, each street an entity. A street would have its outings in summer, the whole village helped in the children's gala, the whole county went to the Miners' Picnic. For the good of all the old days have gone but the disappearing mining village is more than a sign of a dying coalmining industry: it is the end of a way of life and the need to record it is urgent. Already the miners' houses have been bulldozed and pit heaps levelled. In two years the Winning Pit, West Sleekburn, has vanished as though it had never existed. Trees, grass and flowers will soon cover the old ugliness but also the warmth of human life that once was there.

44. Hewers ready to descend Bedlington 'A' Pit, about 1910.
Pitmen working at the face always wore two flannel shirts, the top one of which they removed when hewing, knee length trousers made of cranky flannel or fustian, hand knitted heavy woollen stockings, navy blue or grey in colour, and hobnailed shoes in preference to boots. These hewers are carrying smokey or midgy lamps used while travelling underground in open light mines, candles being employed at the face itself.

45 – 49. These remarkable photographs of work below ground were taken by William Lockey of Bedlington, a pitman, in Sleekburn " A " Pit, about 1910.

45. Stonemen drilling a top caunch with an Elliot patent ratchet drilling machine. The deputy is waiting to charge the drill with explosive.

46. Two stonemen, or ridders, with deputy in the Five Quarter Seam. The roof strata is taken down to make height for a haulage road, the debris being packed under the sides where the coal seam has been removed.

47. Robert Warrier, fore overman, and his son, Edward Warrier, making a survey in the Five Quarter Seam.

48. Hewer, seated on his crackett, kirving or under-cutting in the same seam whilst the deputy watches. The hewer was William Lockey who also took the photograph. He set up the camera, took up position and then gave a signal to a fellow hewer to light the scene by means of magnesium tape.

49. Pitmen about to descend. The shaft examiner is seated on the top of the cage.

50. Thomas Burt, Secretary of the Northumberland Miners from 1865 to 1913, raises a laugh at the annual Miners' Picnic, possibly at Morpeth, 1906.

51. Miners picking coal from waste heaps at Bedlington 'Doctor' Pit during the 1911 Strike.

52. Seaton Delaval Colliery about 1910, a range of pit head buildings typical of the industrial landscape of south east Northumberland. Some of the early prismoid shaped chaldron waggons, each holding 53 cwt. of coal, are among the rolling stock on the colliery railway crossings.

FISHING

The introduction of steam trawlers about 1877 changed the traditional pattern of the Northumberland sea fishing industry. Herrings formerly caught close to land from three or four man cobles – the characteristic boat of the north east coast – were thereafter fished in summer and early autumn off the Northumberland coast or further afield off Ireland or East Anglia, sailing drifters as well as trawlers being used. Gradually as the trawler ports of North Shields and North Sunderland prospered so in Cullercoats, Newbiggin, Boulmer, Craster, Newton and in other smaller havens the industry declined. Following the herring season the trawlers sailed into the North Sea and spent the winter months in the white fish grounds off the Shetlands and as far as Iceland, leaving smaller vessels, known as liners, to work the local grounds. The sailing cobles continued to be used for all kinds of inshore fishing, for line fishing, hooking, sea netting for turbot, inshore netting for sea-trout, for crab and lobster potting, the salmon and sea trout season lasting from February to August.

53. Baiting the lines, Newbiggin on Sea.
Cobles used for line fishing were usually manned by three or four fishermen in partnership and carried seven or eight lines each about 70 fathoms long with between 500 and 1000 hooks baited with one or two mussels. Baiting the lines was consequently a long and tedious task left to the women folk, old men and children at home.

54. Launching a coble, Newbiggin on Sea.
The forward part of the coble is keeled and draws only two or three feet of water but it gradually becomes flat-bottomed towards the after end where it draws practically no water, making it particularly well adapted for beaching.

55. Craster haven about 1880.
Although only a small haven and overshadowed by nearby North Sunderland where the harbour was developed in the 1860s, Craster has established a world wide reputation for kippers. At about the time this picture was taken the Craster fleet numbered as many as twenty seven cobles and about twenty herring drifters. The present harbour was built between 1906 and 1910.

56. Cullercoats fishwives
awaiting the return of the
cobles. In 1905 thirty five cobles
were engaged in salmon and
line fishing at Cullercoats. The
fishwives here, and elsewhere
in Northumberland, wore a
traditional costume comprising
a print bodice, with coloured
neckerchief tucked inside a blue
flannel skirt, worn short and
having a profusion of tucks, home
knitted stockings, and strong
shoes. The wicker baskets,
carried strapped on the shoulder,
were called creels.

57. Sorting herrings at North
Shields Fish Quay.

58. Fishergirls at Blyth gutting and packing herrings in barrels for export to the Continent or the London market.   The girls were probably a party from Scotland who followed the herring boats from port to port and were employed, usually from seven to ten days, when the glut of herrings was landed.   The barrels themselves were brought back from Riga or other Baltic ports.

59. The salmon catch at Tweedmouth.
For the taking of salmon, inshore stake nets and drift nets were commonly employed. This scene looks across to Berwick, the famous Bridge built 1610-34 and the eighteenth-century Town Hall being prominent.   Each fisherman holds a salmon in his hand.

THE TYNE

The Tyne, more than any other name, symbolises the North East. Once the greatest shipbuilding port in the world, the Tyne was equally the main artery through which immense quantities of coal from Northumberland and Durham pits were exported the world over as well as the products of the iron, chemical, engineering, lead, glass industries and of the multitude of other manufactories which concentrated along its ten double miles of bank.

The Tyne in its history inseparably links Durham, Newcastle and Northumberland but it belongs to none and deserves its own special photographic record. Here it is only possible for Northumberland to acknowledge its ties with the river and to say " The Tyne is another story ".

60. Cunard R.M.S. " Mauretania " escorted by two ocean going tugs, numerous steam paddle tugs and a variety of smaller craft, passing North Shields on leaving the Tyne on 22nd October 1907.
Built at the Wallsend Yard of Swan, Hunter & Wigham Richardson, the " Mauretania ", 32,000 tons and 790 feet in length, was then the largest and most luxurious vessel in the world. Immediately it claimed the blue riband for the fastest Atlantic crossing and proudly ruled the ocean until eventually succeeded by the " Queen Mary " in 1935.

61. A three masted vessel, possibly a whaler converted to steam, passing North Shields. The square tower is Low Lights, which, with another tower, High Lights further up the steep bank, up to the middle of the 19th century provided mariners with their main bearings for navigating the entrance to the Tyne between the notorious Black Midden rocks on the north and the Herd Sands on the south.

62. Albert Edward Dock, built in 1884 by the Tyne Improvement Commissioners. Constituted in 1850, the Commission gradually transformed the river from a tortuous shallow stream, fordable at Newcastle where vessels lay aground against the quayside at low tide, into a modern deep water port. This view, taken about 1890 when steam was rapidly replacing sail, looks south east. The harbour entrance from the Tyne may be seen between the masts of the sailing vessel off-loading pit props in the foreground, while among other points of interest are the five-storey grain warehouse and the Training Ship " Wellesley " which may be glimpsed in the background over the right end of the passenger railway station for seamen and immigrants.

QUARRYING

63.   Little Mill limestone quarry, Long Houghton.
The bowler hatted gentleman is John Richardson, the owner, who also worked the extensive nearby whinstone quarry whence roadstone and lime produced in the large kilns were conveyed directly on to the main railway line at Little Mill.   The traction engine was horsedrawn.

64.   Quarry workers at Little Mill whinstone quarry which at one time employed up to one hundred men.   Quarrying still remains a large industry in the county.

JOINERS AND CARTWRIGHTS

65. Interior of the joiners' shop, Bedlington Co-operative Society.

66. Bedlington cartwrights displaying the tools of their trade and the parts of a cart or wain before assembly.

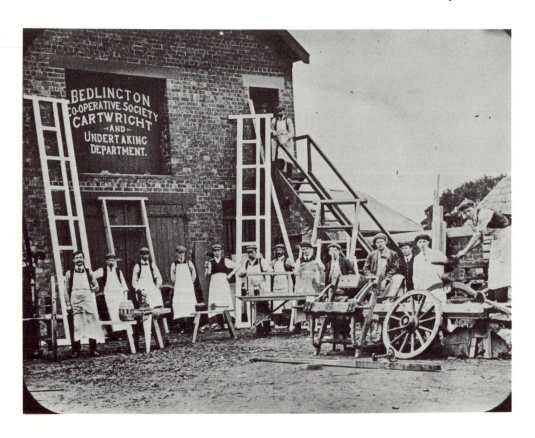

HORSEDRAWN TRANSPORT

In 1890 practically every wheeled vehicle was horsedrawn and it would take a carriage maker's catalogue to distinguish by name all the types to be seen on the road. So far as the country districts were concerned the picture would not have changed much even by 1910 but in the towns it was a very different story. Now, added to the old mixture of carts, gigs, cabs, brakes, omnibuses, waggons and waggonettes, there was an ever increasing variety of motor vehicles, not to mention on Tyneside, at least, the trams, all competing for road space, all travelling at differing paces and emitting discordant noises, and altogether causing the same sort of congestion we see today.

67. The " Chevy Chase " coach crossing Ponteland old bridge about 1899.
The opening of the main line railways in the 1830s and 1840s brought to a rapid end the age of long distance travel by coach. Although local coaches continued to serve the country districts beyond the reach of the railways until the advent of the motor omnibus, this coach is probably a special run to commemorate the famous " Chevy Chase " coach which ran from Newcastle to Edinburgh via Carter Bar for some years after the main road, the present A696, was improved by the Ponteland Turnpike Trust in 1830.

68. A private party setting out from Cragside in a four wheeled dogcart or trap drawn by two horses.

69. Mitford Choir outing, 1911. The brake would have been hired to convey the party probably only as far as Morpeth Station for an excursion further afield. The three storey building in the background is the Plough Inn.

70.   The country bus.
Although much less smartly
turned out than the Mitford
brake, at least this ' omnibus '
gave its passengers some
protection from the weather.

71.   A variety of horsedrawn
vehicles drawn up outside the
Nags Head, Morpeth, probably
on market day.

The Nags Head, whose gables
lent so much character to
Newgate Street, although in
appearance seventeenth century
was in fact built in the
19th century.

72. Blackett Street, Newcastle upon Tyne, in the days of the horsedrawn bus and tram. The Mechanics Institute and Central Library buildings in New Bridge Street which were taken down to make way for the new Central Library in 1969 are in the distance, and nearer to Northumberland Street on the same side is the Unitarian Chapel, the twin turrets of which now distinguish St. Charles R.C. Church in Gosforth.

73. The Newcastle to Kirk-whelpington Royal Mail coach which was robbed on the highway near Kenton in 1905, standing outside the Kenton Post Office.

At first the letters were collected from and delivered to the Rothbury and Alwinton mounted rural postman who called at Hepple each morning and evening. As postmaster, Mr. Clark received £3 a year later raised to £5 in 1874, from which time he had to go to Flotterton to meet the mounted postman. Apart from Hepple itself, he covered 22 miles either on foot or by pony and trap in his daily postman's " walk " which took in Hepple Whitfield, Hepple Woodside, Flotterton and Caistron, for which he received the princely weekly allowance of 18/6d.

74. John Clark, postmaster at Hepple from 1869 to 1902 when he retired at the age of 80 years.

TRAINS AND TRAMS

At the turn of the century all of Northumberland's branch lines were fully worked: Haltwhistle to Alston, Hexham to Allendale Town, the Border Counties from Hexham to Riccarton, the Wansbeck Valley, Scots' Gap to Rothbury, Alnwick to Cornhill and Berwick, and the North Sunderland Railway. All, except only the Alston line, have long since closed, and their tracks are now little more than overgrown paths. In their day the railways provided something never previously enjoyed by country people – cheap, speedy and reliable transport. The housewife could now shop in Newcastle or the local town, goods reached new markets, farmers could send livestock in prime condition, people lived further from their work, and families could enjoy a picnic at the coast or in the country, and have a holiday at the seaside.

75. The Birthplace of the Railway!
An early Stephenson locomotive originally built in 1830, re-built in 1867, still working at Killingworth Colliery, about 1875. This engine, called " Billy " was presented to Newcastle Corporation in 1881 to mark the centenary of George Stephenson's birth. It stood at the end of the High Level Bridge until 1896 when it was moved to the Central Station.

76. Express approaching Plessey Station crossing at speed, 1898.

77. Glanton Station on the Alnwick to Cornhill branch of the North Eastern Railway opened in 1887.

78. Steam excavator at work on the construction of the Ponteland railway in 1904. Although many of Northumberland's branch lines and major railway improvements were constructed during the lifetime of the camera, very few photographs were made showing work in progress.   Even today recording is still left to the amateur.

79. Horsedrawn trams at Gosforth waiting to carry racegoers returning from Gosforth Park back to Newcastle, while a fully loaded brake passes the old Queen Victoria Inn, 1894. The partially built Council Offices places the scene at the present junction of Church Road and the High Street as well as dating the photograph. The Newcastle-Gosforth route was the main section of the Newcastle Corporation's first tramway in 1878. Until 1901 the trams were drawn by horses but by 1904 all the City's main routes had been electrified.

80. Passengers transferring from trams operated by the Tyneside Tramways Company to the Corporation trams at the Henry Street terminus, Gosforth, during Race Week, 1904. Between them, the Corporation, the Tyneside, and the Tynemouth Tramway companies covered the whole of north Tyneside, from Whitley Bay to Throckley. Tramway systems were also planned, but never built, from Morpeth to Bedlington, and in Ashington and Blyth.

THE MOTOR CAR

When most of the photographs in this album were taken the motor car was still largely the plaything of the well to do. However, severe tests such as the RAC 1000 miles rally conclusively proved its reliability and few could have doubted that the motor was the private transport of the future.

81. Walter Christy's motor proudly displayed to the camera of his brother-in-law, Canon R. C. Macleod, at Mitford, 1908.

82. Motor car, admired by schoolboys, leaving the local coach standing outside the Five Stars, Ponteland, about 1905.

83. Ladies of the Mitford choir clambering aboard their Newcastle charabanc, possibly an Albion, at Kelso. They seem to be well prepared for, if not anticipating with pleasure, fifty odd miles of dusty travel on rough country roads in an open, unsprung, solid wheeled vehicle.

The motoring outfit of the day was what would nowadays be politely called " sensible wear ". It mainly comprised a long loose dustcoat, a veil tied over the fashionable large brimmed hat and often goggles to protect the traveller from dust and glare.

84. An early " minibus ", with chain drive, different size wheels, oil lamps and other primitive design features, conveying a party to Alnmouth, about 1910.

LEISURE AND SPORT

Although seventy years ago people worked much longer hours than today they still found plenty of zest for hard physical games and for organised sport. Without question the greatest sporting day of the year was Plate Day in Newcastle Race Week, while meetings were held regularly at Hexham, Morpeth and Rothbury. In the country the hunt was followed with general excitement, not least by the schoolchildren who risked a caning for playing truant to see the huntsmen go by. Obstacle races, running and wrestling were common in country sports while few party outings were complete without some hastily arranged races for grown-ups and children alike.

85. The angler, near Grubbit Mill.

86. Whitley Bay beach, 1905.
The bathing huts were at one time drawn by horse down to the sea to enable the bathing belles, well clad in an ample tunic over ankle length navy blue flannel knickers, to step modestly straight into the water.

87. Residents of Stocksfield will recognise this ford of the Guessburn

88. A quiet game of cricket on the lawn at Mitford vicarage.

89. Mitford village string orchestra at rehearsal in the Vicarage garden.

90. Coursing in Coquetdale.   91. Country boys wrestling.

92. The Panama House Café, the popular teatime resort for outings to Whitley Bay. The café was built about 1888 by Stephen Fry, a retired ocean diver.

He started with a cabin taken out of the ship " Panama " then being repaired at Swan Hunters' and gradually added other cabin walls, floor covering, and curtains, all from different ships, to make a galley, chartroom and large messroom. It even had linoleum as used in the " Mauretania " and, as the photo shows, was decorated with a splendid figurehead of Britannia. After a long and useful life, it was finally taken down in 1934. The building in the background the Prudhoe Memorial Convalescent Home opened in 1869, now also demolished.

93. The annual May Day procession at Rothbury.

94. James Johnston, schoolmaster, bandmaster and organiser of the procession.

95. William Green, the Duke's piper.

96. The Northumberland Scouts being inspected at Thropton by Baden-Powell accompanied possibly by J. M. Carter who was the scoutmaster at the time, about 1910.

97. The start of the annual Rothbury and district road race.

98.   The Northumberland Huzzars Imperial Yeomanry in field dress breaking camp at Rothbury Racecourse following their return from South Africa, 1902.

99.   The Yeomanry, under the command of Colonel J. B. Cookson, marching in full dress through Rothbury on church parade, 1902.

100. Lord Armstrong, the industrialist and benefactor of Newcastle, in the porch of Cragside near Rothbury.

101. Old William Crozier, Coquetdale shepherd, with his collie.

102. A quiet drink and a chat about old times, Rothbury, about 1880.

103. The "Dutchman", who made a living by catching eels, standing at the gate of his cottage near Bedlington.

104. "Coffee Tommy", a tramp well known on the Ponteland Road in the 1890s.

105. Cottagers at Bardon Mill. Although this picture comments starkly on the primitive conditions of the cottager's life, yet the photographer has sensed the dignity of a well earned rest after a hard life. The man's obviously precarious hold on his stool provides a touch of humour. Doubtless, an animated conversation took place after the picture was taken – perhaps a timely reminder that the camera cannot tell the whole story.